A Special Gift

for:

....

from:

....

date:

....

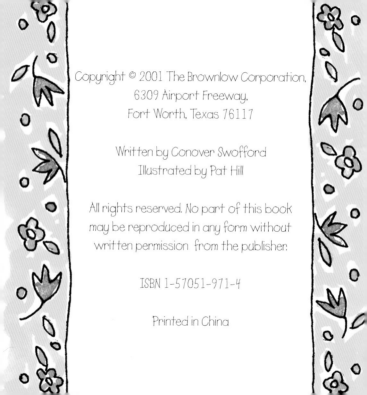

75 Ways
To Be Good To Yourself

WRITTEN BY
Conover Swofford

ILLUSTRATED BY
Pat Hill

Brownlow

Little Treasures Miniature Books

75 Ways to Be Good to Yourself

75 Ways to Calm Your Soul

75 Things to Do With a Friend

75 Ways to Spoil Your Grandchild

A Little Book of Blessing

A Little Book of Love

A Little Book for Tea Lovers

A Roof with a View

Baby's First Little Book

Baby Love

Baby Oh Baby

Catch of the Day

Dear Teacher

For My Secret Pal

Friends

The Gift of Friendship

Grandmother

Happiness Is Homemade

Happy Birthday

How Does Your Garden Grow

How to Be a Fantastic Grandmother

Love & Friendship

Mom

Sisters

Tea Time Friends

They Call It Golf

1. Calm your spirit
by watching fishes swim
and butterflies flutter.

2. Watch the funniest movie you can think of. The laughter will do you good.

◆◆◆

3. Put on your favorite dance music and dance—it's great exercise and very uplifting.

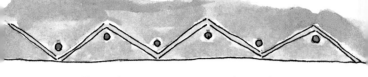

4. Color a picture with a child. It's best if you use the biggest box of crayons you can find.

5. Be still and listen to God speak in your heart.

6. Smile at yourself often in a mirror.

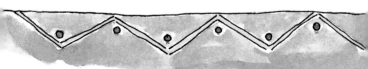

7. Start a Happiness Journal. Every time something makes you happy, make note of it in your journal. Whenever you're sad, read the entries in your journal. It'll make you feel better.

8. Forgive someone who has done you wrong. Make peace with the incident and move on.

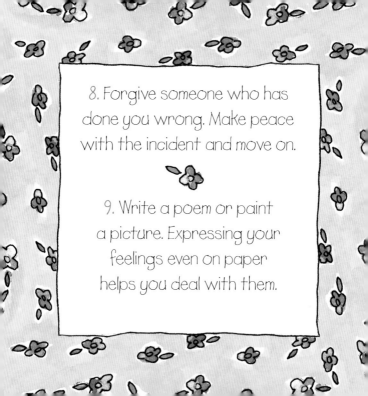

9. Write a poem or paint a picture. Expressing your feelings even on paper helps you deal with them.

10. Stretch. It will relieve tension, relax your muscles, and make your whole body feel good.

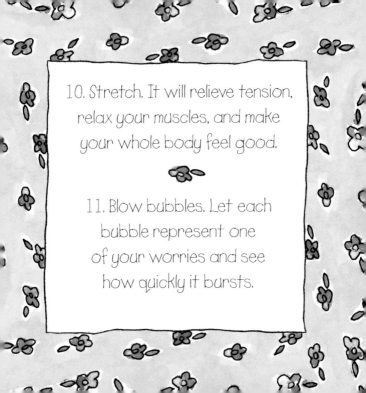

11. Blow bubbles. Let each bubble represent one of your worries and see how quickly it bursts.

12. Pick wildflowers. If you don't have a field of daisies handy, buy yourself a bouquet at the local market.

13. Spend time with the best memories you have. Allow yourself to remember something that inspired you or made you happy.

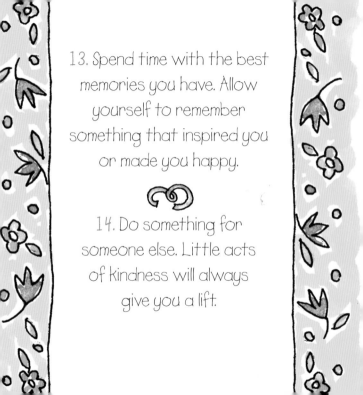

14. Do something for someone else. Little acts of kindness will always give you a lift.

15. Make a blessings jar:
Every time that you are blessed.
Put a pebble in the jar.
Every time that you are blue.
Count your "pebble" blessings so far.
In time you'll come to realize
Instead of tripping you,
God put these pebbles in your path
To help and bless you through.

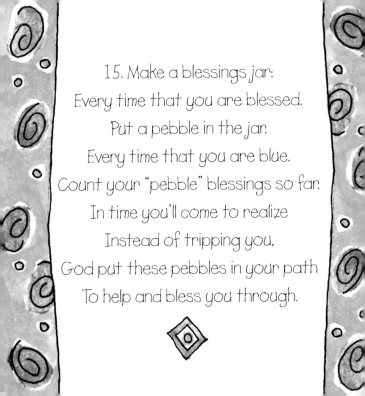

16. Plant a garden. It will bless you and everyone who sees it.

17. Send someone a funny, inspirational, or encouraging card. Picking it out will lift your spirits as well.

18. Find a scent you like—perfume, candle, potpourri—and keep it near you.

19. Eat ice cream and
have a long chat
with your best friend.

20. Don't listen to other
people's criticisms.
Do what's right for you.

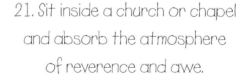

21. Sit inside a church or chapel
and absorb the atmosphere
of reverence and awe.

22. Make a Kindness Box.
Every time someone does
something nice for you,
write it on a 3x5 card and
put it in your box.
Whenever you feel low,
read your cards, and see
how nice people really are.

23. Start a prayer journal.
Keep a list of your prayer
requests—the dates you
made them and the dates
they were answered.
The results will amaze you.

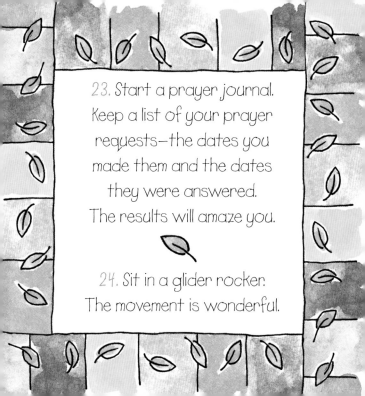

24. Sit in a glider rocker.
The movement is wonderful.

25. Put a bird feeder where you can see it through a window and watch the birds and squirrels play.

26. Start a charm bracelet. Choose charms that remind you of wonderful things and then wear it as a constant reminder of things that make you happy.

27. Get cozy with one of
your favorite books.

28. NO thyself—practice self-denial. Don't try to do it all. Learn to say "no." Knowing your limitations is a sign of maturity, not a lack of perseverance.

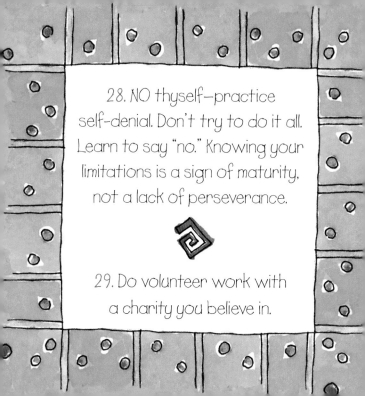

29. Do volunteer work with a charity you believe in.

30. Go to the local animal shelter and adopt a pet. If you want something to wait on hand and foot, get a cat. If you want unconditional love, get a dog. If you want to scare the neighbors and keep burglars away, get a snake.

31. Remove yourself from stressful situations you can't change. Sit on a park bench and feed the birds—you'll be amazed at how soothing this is.

32. Treat yourself to a
day at a spa, or at least have
a manicure or pedicure.

33. Pick a career you are
suited for and that you like.
When you enjoy your job,
life seems a little easier.

34. Freshen up a room in your home—paint, paper, or just change the drapes. If you're on a budget, try rearranging the furniture and adding a throw pillow or two.

35. Adjust your attitude.

36. Look at all the things in your home that were gifts. Take time to remember who gave you the gift, on what occasion, and why. Realize you have decorated your home with the love of others.

37. Hug someone you love.

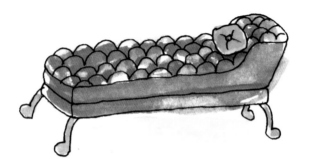

38. Take a nap or just lounge for a while. God created rest to benefit us.

39. Remember there's only one person in the whole world who can truthfully say, "No one is worse off than me," and thank the Father that it isn't you.

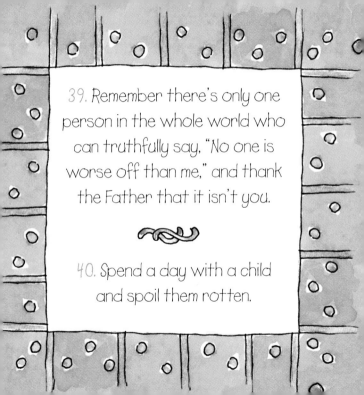

40. Spend a day with a child and spoil them rotten.

41. Get the most comfortable mattress and pillow you can find for yourself. Never underestimate the value of a good night's sleep.

42. Research a subject that interests you. Expanding your knowledge expands your horizons.

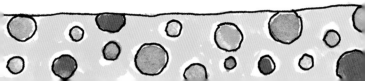

43. Watch the sunset and think about how differently God paints the sky every day for your special enjoyment.

44. Get a new hairstyle. It's amazing how changing your hairstyle can boost your spirits.

45. Congratulate everyone you can for any reason you can. The more you acknowledge other's efforts, the more you'll see the good in the world around you.

46. Learn from everything that comes your way. Looking for the lesson is what turns defeat into opportunity.

47. Listen to your favorite music. Go to a concert or perform one yourself.

48. Rediscover the child in you.
Think of something fun you did as
a child and do it again. (Don't worry;
if you get stuck up the tree, the
fire department will rescue you.)

49. Try a new recipe—an elaborate
dessert; an interesting main dish,
something from another culture.

50. Go for a car ride in the country on an autumn day. Look at the lovely fall foliage. Stop somewhere for freshly made apple cider.

51. Build a snowman or start a snowball fight. Then come home and treat yourself to a steaming cup of hot cocoa.

52. Watch the moon come up.
Try to count the stars and
realize that the God who
created them also created you.
And you are truly special.

53. Play fetch with a dog
(be sure you do your share
of the fetching).

☆

54. Take a continuing education
class and learn how to do
something new and different.

☆

55. Accept compliments. Realize
that you do deserve them.

56. Plan a slumber party for just yourself. Rent several movies that you have been wanting to see, pop popcorn, and curl up on the sofa with a big blanket.

57. Help deliver Meals On Wheels or help out in a soup kitchen for the homeless. You can meet some fascinating people.

58. Take time each day just for you to refresh and renew. Drink a cup of hot tea and read a meditation or just meditate on your own. Renew your spirit.

59. Get in touch with nature. Go horseback riding or mountain biking. In the winter try cross-country skiing or rent a snowmobile.

60. Give yourself a foot massage every night. Rubbing your feet with peppermint lotion will make tired feet feel refreshed and put a little pep in your step.

61. Join a club. Many places have wonderful clubs where you can meet people and/or provide needed services to the community.

62. Pick your battles carefully. You can't fight them all so save your energy for the ones that are truly important.

63. Visit an art gallery
or museum. Looking at
paintings and sculpture
can be inspirational.

64. Read aloud your favorite Bible passage or inspirational text.

◆◆◆

65. Take a mini vacation. Stay overnight or for the weekend in a local hotel or bed and breakfast. Get away from your phone.

66. Have a good cry.
Sometimes you just need one.

67. Find something that is good for you that you actually like. It could be something nutritional to add to your diet or a new form of exercise.

68. Only wear comfortable shoes.

69. Don't hold yourself to impossible standards. God doesn't.

70. When you're sick, stay home and pamper yourself. No one where you work wants your germs anyway.

71. Take a walk in the rain. Get soaking wet. Then come home and take a hot shower.

12. Listen to classical music while relaxing in a bubble bath. Add lavender oil. The aroma is calming.

73. Get a massage. If you can't afford the local spa package, try a massage school instead. They are less expensive and can be quite wonderful.

74. Choose clothes in colors that make you feel good just looking at them.

75. Take a walk through a forest or a garden and be amazed at the beauty in every detail, every sound, and every gentle breeze.

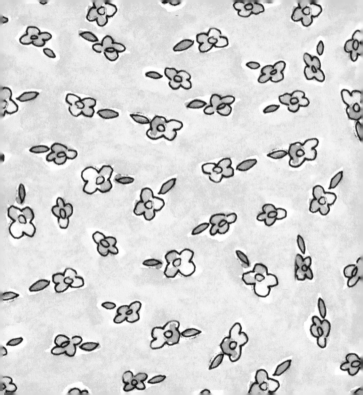